Between Two Moons

Also by Judith E.P. Johnson

Mountain Moods (VDL Publications, 1997)
Gatherers (VDL Publications, 1998)
Fragments (VDL Publications, 2000)
Selected Poems CD (7 RPH, 2001)
Snapshot (Regal Press, 2003)
Landmarks (Ginninderra Press, 2005)
Alone at the Window (Ginninderra Press, 2012)
Waking from Dreams (Ginninderra Press, 2016)

Judith E.P. Johnson

Between Two Moons
haiku & senryu

Acknowledgements

Special thanks are due to Peter Macrow for his kindness and inspiration; to my children Karen, Debra and Craig for their encouragement and support; to Lyn Reeves for editing this book; and to Ron Moss for designing the cover.

The author's haiku and senryu have been published in *Famous Reporter*, *Tasmanian Times*, *poam*, *paper wasp*, *Blue Giraffe*, *Shamrock*, *Windfall*, *Haiku Oz*, *Prospect*, *Still Heading Out*, *Kō*, *Poetic Reflections* and *Poetry Matters*.

Between Two Moons: haiku & senryu
ISBN 978 1 74027 988 8
Copyright © text Judith E.P. Johnson 2015

First published 2015
Reprinted 2016

GINNINDERRA PRESS
PO Box 3461 Port Adelaide 5015
www.ginninderrapress.com.au

For Graeme

first bloom of spring
high in magnolia leaves
full moon

fallen foxgloves
a cap
for each finger

cobwebs and moss
the wren's nest
in the prickly wattle

birdsong
a kitten in the grass
catches a leaf

face aglow
five-year-old
blows out her candles

loud family discussion
the dog
joins in

fluttering
in my ear
the child's whisper

grandchild gone
I find the silver shoes
beside my slippers

after the car wash
on the rear-vision mirror
the spider's new web

spring clouds
apple tree in full bloom
on my china teacup

mountain view
at my window
lily of the valley

all the lawn daisies
tightly shut –
full moon

Norfolk Island

flying over the Pacific
the sudden sight
of pine trees

welcoming us
at the airport
the Pitcairn language

from the beach
cries
of re-enactment

death of a local –
all the flags
at half-mast

at Burnt Pine
after dark –
full moon the only street light

picking red tomatoes
tang of green leaves
on my hands

sitting under the hedge
a spider and I
share the breeze

so many cherry plums
at the deserted house
I pick childhood jam

tattoo
on the strong man's arm
I love Mum

after the storm –
the dog
from behind the couch

waiting room doll's house
only the dog
at home

late walk home
the aroma
of other people's dinners

playing his trumpet
the young Chinese musician
speaks my language

amongst Christmas lights
the tiny nativity
carved in Bethlehem

balcony
dinner for two
just the moon and I

from Japan
all these butterflies
on my new kimono

across the sunlit table
a ripple
of curtain shadows

at last
in the rear-vision mirror's web
a fly

driving through dark trees
the sunset
flashes on and off

beachside shack
opening a window
I let in the sea

night shallows
I moor the boat
in stars

midnight camp
a cup of moon-chilled water
from the stream

New Year fireworks
we sit beneath
falling stars

after the party
the music
in my feet

between two moons the sun

Lake Dobson National Park

forest canopy
manferns brush
the car windows

mid-day
walking around the tarn
I circle the sun

remnants of the Ice Age
pandani
amongst snow-gums

tourist
hurrying along the track
the black snake

late afternoon
sunlit swarm
of deciduous beech leaves

sunrise
light shines
through the keyhole

making tea
in the sunlit kitchen
my shadow does the same

grey clouds
across the bay
migrating mutton birds

vase of feathers
all the colours
of the sky

family photos
passed round the table
old stories

across the dunes
covering my tracks
the wind

twilight
everyone I meet
is a ghost

wet night
listening to recorded
frog songs

march heatwave –
even the shivery grass
is still

leafy vine
over my fence
a handful of grapes

long run
the old dog
in the cyclist's backpack

April gust
flying out of grasses
winged seed

slanting rain
the gutter
full of acorns

autumn sunshine
gold lights
in your grey hair

adult children
laugh at their young selves
in old photos

morning darkness
in the house
dawn at every window

still hand-in-hand
we return to old haunts
Honeymoon Bay

after the downpour
across Mt Amos
a double rainbow

midnight
a boat in the bay
drifts across the moon

potpourri
scent of flower beds
in the linen cupboard

along the beach
the wind
from mountain snow

scent of spring
in a flowerless garden
mother's new perfume

blue sky
after snow clouds
the white mountain

on the concrete
our kitten's pawprints
twenty years ago

winter breakfast
the taste
of summer honey

cold day
around my neck
the baby's warm hug

first fire of winter
blue smoke curls
in falling snow

winter moon
I put on
my cherry blossom perfume

alone in the surgery
the patient shakes hands
with the skeleton

how red
the Japanese maple
in the cold garden

evening brilliance
I watch the mountain
cover the sun

Under the Mountain

missing you
I rearrange the ornaments
again

alone in the kitchen
I hum the songs
we danced together

sitting in the sun
the dog and I
beside your empty chair

Candle-Glow bottlebrush
given for your seventieth
blooms again

under the mountain
at Cornelian Bay
you wait for me

www.ingramcontent.com/pod-product-compliance
Lightning Source LLC
Chambersburg PA
CBHW062207100526
44589CB00014B/1998